Psalms of My Soul

Gabreael

Live in love + light!
Gabreael

Copyright © 2012 Gabreael

All rights reserved.

ISBN: **146638056X**
ISBN-13: **978-1466380561**

DEDICATION

This book is dedicated to my husband and son who love me unconditionally and encourage me in all that I do.

CONTENTS

	Acknowledgments	7
1	Allow Me	9
2	To Believe	19
3	To Submit	29
4	To Receive	41
5	Time to Act	49
6	Manifesting	55
7	Producing More	63
8	Giving Thanks	71
9	The Power of Joy	83
10	Forgiving Yourself Sets Your Soul Free	97
11	Your Inner Voice Speaks	103
12	Time To Write Your Story	117

ACKNOWLEDGMENTS

This book is a work of love from me to each of you. It shows the inner workings of my mind, body, and soul. How I cope at times in what seems like an ever darkening world. On my meditations, affirmations, and exercises you may need to tailor them to suite your own personal needs. I see meditations and affirmations simply as exercises for the soul, as an unexercised soul is an unhealthy soul and eventually it takes its toll on the physical mind.

I see the soul as an artist, it never speaks, it simply paints its portrait and you are that portrait. If you are unhappy with that portrait own it, and change it.

1 ALLOW ME

Allow me to accept goodness and the divine into my life.

Allow me to accept goodness and the divine into my life.

Allow me to walk forth in this day in love and light.

Allow my light to shine for all to see.

Allow me to be a beacon for those in darkened seas.

Amen

Before you can walk in love and light, you must first allow yourself to do so.

I sit and listen to her weeping, asking questions. The same questions I've been hearing almost daily recently, "Gabreael, am I where I'm supposed to be in my life?" "Am I fulfilling my purpose on this planet?" "Am I doing *what I should be?*"

The fact that she is asking me the question tells me that she probably is. People who wander off their chosen path rarely acknowledge it, let alone question it. Then I give her my best advice; start your day with a simple prayer and/or meditation. The one I use is at the beginning of this chapter.

My morning prayer is only three simple sentences, but they are life-changing sentences. If only we could all practice these three simple ideas, what a different world we would see. Please let my morning prayer inspire you. You can use it as is or alter it to your individual taste (including changing Amen to however you usually end your prayers or meditations).

Perhaps you are still healing, in that case this may resonate more with you

Allow me to accept your love and light on this day,

Allow me to feel your love and light,

Allow others to see me shine with the love and light I am just beginning to feel.

When we take the focus off ourselves and focus it on others, we will begin to see what our purpose in this world really is. Whenever we give freely to others, we give to ourselves. Note that I used the word "Freely." If you give because of guilt or resentment, you are sabotaging any good deeds that you are doing.

When guilt is your motivation for giving, you are allowing events from the past to control your future. If you give under these circumstances, you turn giving into a form of self-punishment. Giving should never be a punishment. Resentment is a form of anger. It can fester and darken the soul. Letting resentment into your life lets others have a hold over you.

These are two different ways to release resentment:

Allow your holy light to ascend upon me, cleansing me, releasing me of all resentment.

Allow me to be kind to those who have wronged me.

Allow me to always be guided in compassion toward others.

Amen

Alternative:

May your light flow upon me and through me, cleansing me, releasing me of all resentment and negativity.

Help me to be kind to those who have wronged me.

Help me to be compassionate towards others.

Allow me to see when you have bestowed your gifts and help upon me.

Allow me to accept your gifts and the help that you offer.

So mode it be.

An old friend called me the other day. She wanted to know if she had destroyed her life by marrying the wrong person. You cannot make a wrong decision; you can only make a decision. It is important to know that if you make a decision and change your mind, you can always make a new decision. Your major life decisions are not accidental. They are lessons that you have chosen and placed in your soul's chart. These are things that you or those around you, have chosen to learn (or teach) in this lifetime.

Before we were born on this plane, we map out our life's chart. You can think of it as being kind of like a blueprint. This chart includes things like your major life path, minor life path, your major lifetime obstacle and minor lifetime obstacle.

These choices include but are not limited to our family birth placement, children, education, health, spouse(s)...Your Higher Power is not sitting above you striking you down with lightning bolts. However, sometimes it may be easier to believe that, than to believe you did this to yourself. Remember that you chose these things, the good, the bad and the ugly, as learning experiences to add to your soul. AS it is in the stormy seas of life where our tattered sails are sculpted for all the world to see.

Below is my personal meditation exercise for knowing the divines will in my life:

1. *Say an opening prayer based on your own personal belief system. I use "The Lord's Prayer."*

Our Father who art in Heaven.

Hallowed be thy name.

Thy kingdom come.

Thy will be done.

On earth as it is in heaven.

Forgive me my debts as I forgive my debtors.

Lead me not into temptation.

Protect me from the evil ones.

Amen

On the other hand, you may be more comfortable with this alternative

God and Goddess I call upon you,

To watch over me

And guide me on this day.

Help me to treat others,

As I would like to be treated.

Protect me and keep me from harm.

2. Then ask that your purpose be revealed to you. Envision your ideal of the hereafter/heaven.

3. See yourself basked in white light.

4. Lay quietly for a few minutes, listen, and look for your purpose to be revealed.

Meditation has been portrayed in the past as something reserved for mystics. Prayer is speaking to the divine. Meditation is simply waiting for a response.

Affirmations for this chapter:

I allow good things to come into my life

I allow good people to be in my life.

You chase away fears, troubles and doubts,

When you allow the light in,

Sometimes, that's all that counts.

2 TO BELIEVE

Before anything can be, you have to think and believe it will be.

Believing you believe in me makes me believe in myself.

Believing in myself makes, others believe in me.

Believing makes me whom I am today in order to show others the way.

Amen

Since you are now allowing yourself to open up to the divine you must believe you can have a better life.

Believe it or not, life is eternal. The Spirit is energy, and energy never dies, it simple transforms. People tend to fear death and they should not because death is simply a form of transition. We need all of the time we have here in this plane, but when that time is over, we simply move on. How you live your life today not only determines where you will be tomorrow, but in the hereafter as well.

One day in church a man stood up in front of me and said, "I don't care how I get to heaven. Even if I am a just a janitor there, as long as I make it is all that matters." I don't know about you, but I have no intention of being anyone's janitor for eternity.

Words are powerful things. A word begins as a thought. Once a word is spoken, it leads to actions. Those actions are what create our experiences in life. In addition, the experiences we have in life are what create our reality.

If you think positive, you will create a positive life. Negative thinking will create a negative life. Even though there are obstacles you have placed in your way, you can overcome them. Your reaction to those obstacles and what actions you take to overcome them determines your future.

It is NEVER too late to change your life for the better. In order to start changing your life, you must start changing your words. To change your words, you must start with changing your thoughts.

When negative thoughts start seeping into your mind stop them and replace them with positive thoughts, prayers and affirmations. Saying affirmations and believing them reshapes our though processes, this in return starts to reshape our lives.

Affirmations assist you in creating a positive energy field around yourself. And while your thoughts alone may not change the world, they will help to change you. It is a big step and maybe one of the hardest, but once your thought process is changed, your life will change. You will see the world differently and the way you move though the world will be different as well. This changes your everyday life and in a way, the world will be changing though you.

A simple activity to help you start actively doing this is listening to your own internal thoughts. When you realize you are thinking about things in a negative way stop yourself and ask, "is that is really true? " If not, then say the opposite thing. If it is true, ask yourself if there is anything you can do to change it. Keep a note and start working towards change.

Regardless of your religious or spiritual views I think the below prayer is a great one when you are working on changing your life.

Grant me the serenity to accept the things I cannot change,
The courage to change the things I can,
And the wisdom to know the difference.

An exercise I have done for years is that every day I choose to appreciate five things about one of the subjects below:

1. Five things about myself.

2. Five things about my husband.

3. Five things about my work.

4. Five things about my family members.

5. Five things about my living space/community.

I firmly believe that each one of us should make our own affirmations list, because each of us is unique. However, here are some examples of affirmations I use for myself:

1. *Five things about myself; I am loved. I am healthy. I am happy. I am at peace. I am beautiful.*

2. *Five things about my husband; I love my husband. My husband loves me. I am happy with my husband. My husband is happy with me. My husband and I complete one another.*

Those are simply a few examples of ones I say for myself. Adjust your own to suit your own life. If you are not married or in a relationship and desire to be in one instead of saying, "I am loved" say, "I am worthy to be loved."

Rome wasn't built in a day, nor was the life you are leading today. Practicing positive thinking, prayers and affirmations may not change your life overnight, but it will help you to change it. Below is an exercise that will help you to keep going, for those times when you feel like you are going nowhere and not making any progress.

Take a note of where you are now. Write down what a day in your life if like. What do you do every day or often? What are your attitudes towards others and events? How do people act towards you? You can be brief, but try to get the essence of your day.

After following the advice in the book for three months, complete this exercise again. You will see a difference in yourself, and how those around you now treat you.

Always remember that the first step in others believing in you is for you to allow yourself to believe in you.

Affirmations for this chapter:

I believe I have good things in my life

I believe my life gets better every day

Gabreael

It's not about fairies,

Though it could be,

It's more about the ability to believe.

Fairies, yourself or a higher power,

When you believe, it doesn't matter.

If you think that good,

Will come your way,

You will see it more every day.

3 TO SUBMIT

To submit you must try hard to understand that while you will not always get what you want when you want it, you will get what you need.

Allow me eyes to see.

Allow me ears to hear.

Allow me to submit without fear.

Amen

You are allowing yourself to believe there is and will be good in your life, now you must submit that there are things beyond your control.

Here is a personal story about an "everyday" submission.

I feel the wind blowing at my body, pulling at my hair, whipping at my feet. It's moist and I know this storm is going to get worse before it gets better. I've picked this time to meditate because there is certain energy in a rising storm; it's something I like to tap into. I hear someone in my front yard yelling for me to get off the roof. My eyes open to see a police officer standing there.

"Why officer? Is there a law against me sitting on my roof?" I ask.

"Look lady there is a hurricane on the way and we have better things to do than answer calls about you sitting on your roof. Please get down." he responds.

After a brief defiance, I submit to the officer's wishes and get down.

The submission of self is without a doubt one of the hardest undertakings one can undergo. Submission is often perceived as being part of domination or as a sign of weakness of character. However, submission is simply the surrender to a higher authority. We surrender all the time in everyday life, starting when we are young. First it is to our parents, then the school system and teachers, after that the justice system...I'm sure you get the idea. Now I am asking you to submit to a higher conciseness than yourself and have faith that it has your greatest good in mind.

Here is another way to look at it. You can pick any activity you truly enjoy, playing sports or going to a game, going to a concert, looking at art or even playing a video game. The possibilities are really almost endless; the secret is to find something you lose yourself in. For this example I am going to use watching a movie, it's something almost everyone does and enjoys.

Let's say you are at the theater, you have your popcorn, drink, maybe your favorite candy. You go in and sit in your favorite spot, the lights dim and the action starts. In the perfect experience you lose yourself in the movie, you don't see the actors as they really are you see the characters they are playing. You become immersed in their world on the screen. For 90 minutes or so, these are your friends and when the movie ends, you are sad to see them go. This is a form of submission.

Now think about the same scenario, but on a bad day, everything is the same, but your frame of mind. Instead of letting go of your worries and becoming immersed in the movie, you are distracted. You are thinking about your bills, the rude comment from a neighbor or the fight with a family member. Even though the film is well written and acted, you do not enjoy it. You don't see the characters on the screen come to life, you see the actors who are portraying them.

This is what happens when you refuse to let go, refuse to open your mind and heart to what could be, when you refuse to submit.

Once we believe we know what the divine has planned for us submitting to it is the next step. When we submit ourselves, we are demonstrating that we believe in a higher power and trust that it will lead us to our best possible selves.

Here is a list of four things that submission to the divine achieves for us:

1. It develops your faith. It is impossible to submit, when you have little to no faith.

2. It teaches us wisdom.

3. It empowers you. When you submit to the divine no one else can have power over you.

4. It allows our will to become one with our

creator.

Always remember the first step to others submitting to your will is for us to submit to the will of the divine.

While you can use the above example with the movie (or any of the suggestions) as an exercise to practice here is another one you should try.

Pick a day with nice weather or at least a day when you can take a walk without the weather being a huge distraction. (Or pick a large indoor area perhaps a mall) Put on some comfortable clothes and shoes you can walk in and go for a walk.

Do not strictly plan your rout; having a general direction in mind is fine, but nothing specific. This will be important later. You can go as slow or fast as you like but try to go at least three blocks away from your starting point and schedule at least 20 minutes of travel time. If needed you can even use some type of transportation like a wheelchair, bike or scooter.

Give yourself about 5 minutes or 1 – 2 blocks to clear your mind. In that time you can think about your worries, problems, plans for the rest of the day, or what has happened in your day so far. After that time is passed, try to wipe all those things from your mind. They may creep back in, don't force them away let it float there for a moment then think of something else and let it float away.

During this next phase, which will be 5 to 10 minutes of your trip, try to be in the here and now. Look around at what is going on. Take note of the trees, flowers and other vegetation as you walk past it. What things do you hear? Cars? Sirens? Birds? Insects? Other animals? Water? Listen for anything you might not normally notice. Feel the air, think about how it feels against your skin, notice the temperature. Is it moist or dry? What else do you notice?

Don't worry about catching everything. The point is to try to catch some things you might normally miss and have not noticed before. The OTHER point is to be in the present and in the moment. Not thinking about the past or the future only thinking about what is going on right now.

The third step is to follow your intuition. If you see a street or path and something says go down there, do it. Do not put yourself in harm's way, but if you can safely go in that direction do. Notice all the things you find on your new rout. Try to take at least one unexpected turn on your adventure. This is the part where you are practicing submission. Submit that and take a turn that maybe you didn't fully choose.

Make sure to watch your time and distance. If you do not get a lot of exercise (or have a set amount of time you can be gone) it might be best to set an alarm to go off half way through the time you want to be gone. That way you will make sure you have both enough time and energy to make it home.

When you are almost back to your house (about a block or 3 - 5 minutes away) think about how you are feeling. What I am hoping for is that you feel happy and light. Unworried and enjoying the sights. You may have other feelings though. Perhaps sad, anxious, angry or any other negative emotion. Though it is not what you are aiming for, this can be normal too. They can come from starting to realize what you have been missing in your life. You may be feeling tired or sore. If it is a physical discomfort that should go away as you get in better shape and do this more often. Nevertheless, make sure not to go as far next time and rest a few days to let your body heal.

Set a limit you are comfortable with. While exercise

does all sorts of great things for you both mentally and physically, that is not what this "exercise" is about.

Affirmations for this chapter:

I submit to the will of the divine.

I do not need to be in control.

Sometimes it's better to go with the flow,

Instead of having to be in control,

Let go of ego and vanity

Just do what's needed,

How hard could it be?

Gabreael

4 TO RECEIVE

To receive what you want, you have to listen to what the divine is telling you and believe you will get it.

To receive your will is my will.

To accept your will is my will.

To live your will is my will.

Amen

Now that you are allowing yourself to believe and submitting to the will of the divine, your next step is to receive what they are sending you.

Its midnight and my eyes pop wide open. I hear a voice say to me, "Wake your husband and pray for John and Jane" (I have substituted their real names). John used to run a prison ministry and Jane is very active at her church. They are an older couple with grandchildren.

They consider themselves prayer warriors, meaning that they regularly prayed fervently for others. To be honest, my first thought was, "Why now and why me?" In that moment, I did not understand why, but I woke my husband up and we prayed for them and their family for about an hour.

This couple's son was a close friend of my husband's at the time, but we had not seen or heard from any of them in weeks. The next morning I got up and went over to John and Jane's. The night before they had been arguing and fighting, with their son over money, property...etc. It had gotten so serious that John had taken out his pistol.

This is a true and simple tale of submitting to the divines will and receiving it. At the time I didn't understand why, but I still did what was requested of me. When you pray or ask for the divine's will to come into your life you must understand that it may take you into unknown waters. Though you may question why, it is into those unknown water that you must sail. When the request comes you may not understand it, but once it is received, submit to it. In time, the reason will be revealed.

I'm often asked when I became psychic. The always seem to expect something like a near death experience, a highly mystical experience or some such thing. I would love to entertain you all with such stories, but I cannot. My mother said that when I was two I started talking to an invisible dog. Evidently, I played with it daily. All I know is that as long as I can remember I knew I could hear the divine, and that the divine, could hear me.

The Creator is our parent. Just as we desire a relationship with our children, the divine desires one with us. My vision of "God" is not as a male or female, therefore I simply refer to it as The Creator. It is The Creator who made the universe and the divine.

Part of receiving what you want, is to know what you want. I am going to give you two different things that can help you decide what these things are. One is a Vision Board, the other is to write a story about what your ideal life looks like. Both of these will help you visualize what you want to you can start making steps to get them in your life.

A Vision Board is simply a collection of pictures of things you would like to have in your life. It can also include words. You can collect these pictures from looking at magazines or catalogs, the internet or by taking your own pictures. It should be used to as inspiration, to remind you of the things you are working towards.

When writing the story you should describe your ideal life. Where you want to live, what you want to do and have. Go into as great of detail as you can. Describe the rooms of your house, the cars you drive, and what you do each day.

Both of these exercises will help you determine what is important in your life and what direction you want your life to go in.

Affirmations for this chapter:

I am open and listen for messages from a higher power.

I believe I will receive the things I want and need.

I believe that I am guided,

By things I cannot see,

I believe in their benevolence,

And that they help me in the life I lead.

I receive their messages and,

The gifts meant for me,

I receive their inspiration,

And that helps me plant the seed.

5 TIME TO ACT

Time to take action and work to attain your goals.

Today I will step forward in action, no matter how great or small the step.

I know that the longest journey starts with one simple step.

Amen

You have allowed yourself to believe there is good in your life, submitted to the will of the divine, and started receiving the messages it sends, it is now time to take action and make things happen.

Now that you have received the divine's will for your life, you will need to start acting upon it. For some this is the hardest step for others it may be the easiest. I have seen many try to implement "The Law of Attraction," into their life with positive affirmations alone, without any form of plan. The obstacle may lie in not knowing or realizing what actions to take.

Here is an example of what I mean. Let us say you want the right person to come into your life. So you create a vision board and put the happy couple at the top of the board. Then instead of going out for a walk every day, or joining a new group, you sit in front of TV every night. You don't go anywhere, never talk to anyone and you expect that person to knock on you door and say "Hi I'm here, take me."

This is not going to work. Instead, you should form a plan of action and start implementing it. If you want to meet someone you need to go out, take some classes, join a meditation or some other type of group...whatever you end up doing, put yourself into places where you will meet a likeminded spouse of character and quality.

To jump start this process I want you to make a list of three to five things you would like to have in your life. Under each of these items, list five things you can do to work towards getting them. Now get to work!

Affirmations for this chapter:

I am active and in motion, surging towards my goals.

Every day I take one-step closer to the life of my dreams.

PSALMS OF MY SOUL

There was once a time,

When I was lonely and sad,

So many things I wanted,

That I didn't have.

Peace of mind and a happy place,

Were on that list,

I felt disgrace.

I picked myself up,

And started that day,

To chase and fight,

That feeling away.

At least one little step each and every day,

Sooner than I'd imagined,

I'd chased my blues away.

Gabreael

6 MANIFESTING

Start bringing what you want into your life.

My soul is at peace.

My mind is at peace.

My home is at peace.

Amen

You have started allowing the divine to help you in your life, you believe it will happen, and have been both submitting and receiving from the divine and are starting to take actions to make your dream life come true. Your next step is manifesting it into your life.

Today is something that you manifested. Every situation, every place you visited and every person you interacted with. I mean this both literally and figuratively, today can be what you did today or it can mean your current state of being in comparison to your past. What really matters is that you know that if you do not like the path your life is currently on in this lifetime you can change it. There is no way that I'm aware of to the past, but you can change your future. Right now, in this very moment you can manifest today, what you desire for tomorrow.

Even if you are content in your life at this time, you can think of ways to improve it for yourself and/or others. I hate using money as an example, but this is an excellent example. I had a client who was a doctor. She was content in her income, but she was worried that she would need extra money because she had just had her first child. Daily she started saying affirmations and implementing them into her life. The last time we spoke, she had doubled her income by simply taking the responsibility for where she was and where she wanted to go.

Manifesting is easy, if you believe it is. When you start doing it consciously, keep things positive and try not to get anxious about your results. Things will happen the way they should and if things do not seem to be working maybe you just need to start a little smaller.

Your first step believes that you will get what you want or what you need. I'm sure there has been something in your life, that somehow right when you needed it most, you got it. That is how manifestation works. *You were manifesting what you needed on a subconscious level, not realizing that you were doing it. Now you are going to make the shift to do this at will.*

Think about what you want. Start out with simple. Like any other skill, this too requires practice to develop your abilities. Let's say what you want is a brand new car. You may want to start with trying to manifest the first $20 towards that down *payment. Then you can move up to $100 and so on. Save the money you manifest towards this purpose, keep the faith and you will get there.*

Starting small will help you gain confidence in yourself and that you can do this.

See yourself holding that first $20. Imagine what it feels and smells like, the texture of the paper. Picture yourself putting it in your pocket, imagine how you will feel when you hold that money and know that it is going towards your final goal. Keep this visualization going for a few minutes.

Hold on to the happy feeling for as long as you can, continue to feel as if you already have the money in your pocket as long as possible. This can help you reach your goal faster. Do this visualization for a few minutes every day and keep an eye out for results.

If you are having trouble figuring out what you want to manifest you can use a simple meditation to help you. Relax and clear your mind as much as possible then ask, "What is the most important thing I need to manifest into my life?" Let the thoughts float into your mind. You may get one distinct answer or you may still have a few. Let the ideas come and go. If you do not have, distinct answers try again another time. Sometimes a little time is needed.

I chose my peace prayer for this chapter because if you do not have peace in your soul, mind and home it is hard to manifest much. In a world at war, we need all the peace we can find.

Affirmations for this chapter:

There is _____ (a positive thing) in my life.

I am a _____ (a positive trait) person.

I have _____ (something good).

Believe that you,

Will get what you need,

Focus and visualize,

I know you can see,

Put forth your intent,

A little each day,

And watch your desires,

Start coming your way.

7 PRODUCING MORE

After manifesting what you need in your life it is important to expand that energy and keep it going.

Heavenly Creator, I thank you for the blessings you have sent to me.

I ask you to help me produce more with the gifts you have helped me to acquire.

Please show me the way to keep brining _____ into my life.

Please show me the best way to help those who need this in their lives as I once did.

Amen

You have allowed good into your life and believed it will keep getting better. You're submitting to the divine's will in your life, receiving its message, and acting upon them. You are manifesting what you want to come into your life and are now going to take those gifts and produce more with them.

Now that you have manifested what you wanted and are where you want to be, you have to produce and do something more with it to keep the energy going. Since you now have an open dialogue with the divine, you are talking and listening to it, and the divine is talking and listening to you, it is time to ask yourself what do I produce with the gifts you have been given? When I say produce, I am talking about producing more with what you have manifested.

This is a story about a friend of a friend; I think it sums up nicely what this chapter is trying to say. Her name is Jane and she worked at a marketing firm making a good living as a consultant. Then 9/11 happened and like many, she realized the discontent she felt at her present job and she quit. She, like many at that time, realized that life can be taken away at any moment and that it is too precious to waste doing something you do not really enjoy.

She had always wanted to start her own business and work with likeminded individuals. Jane got some money together and a partner to help run the business and opened an alternative health center. Along with giving these practitioners a cost effective way to have an office to see their clients in, she also coached them and helped them expand their businesses, making both them and she more money.

Find a quiet place to sit and think about what you are manifesting in your life. Make a list of three things you can do to sustain this in your life and how to improve what you are manifesting to make more.

Next make a list of three ways you can use what you are manifesting to "pay it forward" or improve the situation of another (others) that also needs what you have produced.

Here is a mediation that can help you in this process.

After you have brought yourself to a relaxed state and have generally cleared your mind start thinking about the things you have manifested in your life. You may see a slow movie or it could be flashes of images or anything in between.

Let them go for a few moments then slow them down and clear you mind again. Ask yourself "How can I produce more with what I have manifested?"

Be ready to expand on your ideas, and then start working on putting these new plants into action.

You may be thinking great, I have already done so much, now you are asking me to do more. You should already know this life is a continual journey, so of course there is more for you to do.

You can take a rest and enjoy what you have accomplished, because it really is a lot. Just don't rest too long. Manifesting takes continual energy to keep it going. The divine wants you to keep moving forward. Your best results will happen when you have a continual focus and gradually evolving. Slow and steady really does win this race.

When I needed_____, you gave it to me,

Now help me to keep producing it so

I will have it for both others and myself in need.

Amen

Affirmations for this chapter:

I appreciate what I have achieved, and to honor that, I use it to achieve more in my life.

I am producing more every day.

Every day I look for ways to improve my life and the lives of those around me.

Sometimes you think,

That you are done,

But really, you have just begun.

8 GIVING THANKS

Being thankful for the things in your life helps you appreciate your life and live a happier one

For yesterday, I am thankful.

For today, I am hopeful.

For tomorrow, I am blessed.

While walking in the light and believing in the good fortune you deserve you are submitting to a will beyond yourself and receiving the gifts it offers. Taking action and manifesting your desires has led you to produce the things you need. Now it is time to give thanks for all the gifts in our life.

Giving thanks is so underrated in our society today. I give thanks every morning when my eyes open and every night before my eyes close. No matter what the situation was that day, I always find something to be thankful for. I often hear others saying they have nothing to be thankful for, "So and so has this and that; why do I suffer while they are rewarded?" Obstacles, pain, challenging circumstances are not punishments; they should be looked at as opportunities to learn from. Sometimes, just that opportunity to learn is something to be thankful for.

Higher Power, I want to thank you for all the things I have in my life.

Thank you for my friends and family.

Thank you for helping me every day.

As soon as you realize what you have in your life to be thankful for, and start giving thanks for it, you will start the process of feeling better. No matter what the obstacle or situation, when you give thanks for what you have in your life, you will start attracting goodness into it. The greatest form of thanks is the thanks that are given in difficult circumstances.

When my son was in the service, he suddenly got married to someone he knew we would not approve of. He used the excuse that he wanted to marry her before we met her so regardless of our feeling for her we would have to accept her and the marriage.

Well, a year later he was divorced. You would think he was the only person on the planet to ever go through a divorce. He moved back home and while there we was constantly wallowing in self-pity and pushing the envelope with my husband and I. He did his best to see how much we would take before breaking or abandoning him, neither of which ever happened.

The moral to the story is

 At that point, there were times I didn't think I would make it with him.

During that time I wasn't sure I was going to make it through that phase without breaking. He was horrible, he pushed every button I have drinking, drugs, you name it he did it. Thankfully I realized that he was going through a self-abuse phase and all any of us could do was just love him unconditionally, not condone his behavior, but love him.

Reflecting back years later on that period, I realize that my son taught me about unconditional love during that time. I don't know that I had ever had it before that time, and today I am so thankful for that lesson. I wouldn't trade it for anything. When I was going through it I could not comprehend it, but now I am so thankful for it.

The next few pages are to help you get start and end your days in "Thanks."

Gabreael

This morning I am thankful for :

PSALMS OF MY SOUL

Gabreael

Tonight I am thankful for:

Gabreael

Affirmation for this chapter:

I thank (my higher power) for the wonderful things and people in my life.

I thank my friends and family for their love and support.

I'm more thankful today, than I was yesterday,

For all the things that have come my way.

My yellow brick road,

May have been filled with strife,

But it made me what I am today,

I love my life.

9 THE POWER OF JOY

Don't wish for just a happy life, wish for a joyous one.

Let my life be full of joy

Help me to feel the joys in life instead of just the sorrows

Allow me to bring joy not only to myself, but to the lives of others as well.

Amen

The light is shining upon you and you believe you deserve the good things in your life. While taking charge of life, you are also open to the will of your higher power. You receive the messages that are sent and act in a way that will help you manifest and produce what you need, while remembering to be to be thankful for what you have already received. This thankfulness for what you have will help bring joy into your life.

We give thanks through our acts, but holding on to that state of thankfulness comes by acknowledging the power of "Joy" in our lives. You cannot put your hands, per-say, on "joy" for it is an emotion, and being so, it is an intangible commodity. What you feel is what determines the way you act towards others. In order to do" good" things, you must first feel "good" about yourself and your life.

If you love what you are doing, no one needs to motivate you. You will want to get up and go to work, because it will no longer be work. At least not the way most people think of it. Working aside, all aspects of your life will be happier if you are doing more things that bring you joy.

So, how do you feel good or find joy in a planet that seems to be in a never-ending state of crisis? I see crises as opportunities. See problems as challenges that can be solved. They are an opportunity for transformation of the soul. We all have crises in our life and how we handle them shows the world what kind of sailor we are going to be in the sea of life.

"We are shaped by our thoughts; we become what we think. When the mind is pure, joy follows like a shadow that never leaves."

"Buddha"

I keep a journal at my desk and every day I write a list of five things in it that have brought me joy. They range from watching the sunrise to petting my dogs, losing weight to smelling the flowers. At the end of each week, I also list five joys I have shared with others.

I find I am my happiest when I am sharing with others. It can be as simple as sharing an ice cream float with my husband to sharing my time with a senior in a rest home. Regardless the activity or location I find that I am my happiest when I am sharing with others. Reflecting over all the people I know, I find that those who are the most selfish and self-centered are also the unhappiest people I know.

Joy Meditation

See yourself lying in your favorite space of all time while breathing deeply in and out. You have a joyful feeling of love growing inside of you in your solar plexus area. You feel it growing and spreading throughout the body.

You then see a beautiful white light encompassing you, breathe it in and out, in and out. You feel connected to this light as it engulfs you, you are immersed within it becoming one with the light and you realize that you are one with all.

You then see yourself sending out this light to your friends and family and you realize that you are a conduit for the light in this world. You then slowly feel yourself coming back knowing that you are now one with the light you are now one with the universal consciousness.

Below is not so much an exercise for you to do, as it is a list of suggestions on things you may want to add or change in your life to help you live not only a happy life, but also a joyous one. Because joy is much deeper and longer term emotion and state of being than happiness is.

1) Go outside and appreciate the beauty of nature. Watch a sunrise or set, look at the flowers, trees and other vegetation. Watch birds and other animals in their natural habitats. Relax and watch the water flow or the clouds float by.

2) Bring nature into your environment. It can be cut flowers, some indoor plants or even just pictures of nature scenes. One project is to gather some things from outside and put

them in a decorative bowl. The items could be flowers, herbs, twigs, leaves, rocks…arrange them in the bowl and keep it somewhere you will see it often.

3) Volunteer. This can be formally somewhere for the needy or elderly or just helping a neighbor in need.

4) Turn off the news. Whether it is the TV, radio or online most of the news is depressing and will help to bring you down. This does not have to be permanent, but at least until you are feeling more joy in your life. If you feel the need, have a friend or family member who watches it keep you updated on only the important things that they know will apply directly to you.

5) Bond with family. You might already get together with your family on a regular basis, but if you don't, pick some positive/favorite family members

and visit them more often.

6) If you are having trouble connecting with family or the people around you try reaching out to friends on the internet. You can find old friends or some likeminded new friends online.

7) Connect with your neighbors and/or community. It can be people you live near of just people in your part of town. Having more friends and a strong nearby support system can help counteract feelings of being along and disconnected.

8) Laugh, or at least smile more. It is scientifically proven that smiling (even if it's not real) releases feel good chemicals into your body and that laughter can help fight cancer. So rent a funny movie, go to a comedy club or just make a point of smiling throughout the day.

9) Find an outlet for your anger and rage. Keeping emotions in is never a good thing, especially negative emotions. Exercise, write or talk it out with an understanding friend. Whatever you do, find a way to release and overcome those emotions.

10) Find something that makes you happy and joyful. I have known a few people in my lifetime that had a much easier time knowing what they did not like than knowing what they did. While knowing what you don't like is a step in the right direction, having things you do like to do, is a much better one. Try things you haven't done before and talk to new people. At the very least, you will have some new stories to share with your friends and know a few more things that you do not want to try again.

11) Reduce you stress. Make a list of things that are stressors in your life and figure

out how to relieve all or at least some of them.

12) Take the time to develop your spirituality. Learn more and do more to connect with your higher power and other aspects of your chosen religion.

13) Have a really good meal. I don't know about you, but I love to eat really good food. Making a point of having a good meal makes you feel better about yourself because you are telling your inner voice that you are taking the time to do something good for yourself.

14) Head off problems by planning ahead. It can be simple like picking out your clothes the night before so you aren't rushed in the morning, or paying bills on time so you don't have late fees. Taking a drive or planning a day trip? Pack a jacket and shorts so you will be comfortable no matter what the weather at your destination. These are just a

couple examples I am sure there are thousands of little things you can do to help cut down stress, that you might not even realize are stressors.

15) Find a special connection or activity with the special people in your life. Maybe it's yard selling with your Aunt, drinking coffee with your mom, going to the movies with your best friend, going rafting with your cousin or watching a favorite TV show and discussing it with your husband. Find something that you and those people special to you both like to do and do it together.

16) Complement yourself. Tell yourself you are great or did a good job. If needed, make a list of things you like about yourself or what you do, and tell yourself once a day.

17) Ask for help when you need it, you may

find you don't have to do it all alone.

18) Don't worry about things you cannot control. Ask yourself if there is anything you can do about the situation, if the answer is no, let it go.

19) Do not try to be perfect, no one is, regardless of how they may look on the outside.

20) Take care of yourself! Try to eat well, get exercise, and take care of your basic needs. You would be surprised how many people don't take care of their selves. Always remember you can't take care of anyone else if you don't take care of yourself first. Sometimes that may include talking to a therapist. They can help you see things about your life and what about it that is bothering you that you have trouble seeing on your own.

Affirmations for this chapter:

I have joy in my life.

I bring joy to others.

Joy in your heart,

Joy in your mind,

Joy in your life,

Until the end of time.

10 FORGIVING YOURSELF SETS THE SOUL FREE

Forgiveness is an essential step in healing your life, but sometimes it's easier to think of it as changing your direction.

God and Goddess hear my plea,

Grant me the ability,

To forgive those who have hurt me.

Amen

You are allowing goodness to flow into your life and believing that only more will come to you. Allowing yourself to be open to the will of the divine is helping you to receive the messages that are being sent. Taking action in your life has helped you to manifest and produce what you've been missing in your life. Being thankful and learning to find joy in your life has brought you to the point where you can forgive yourself, which will set you free.

Forgiving yourself starts with forgiving others, understanding that people make mistakes and make bad decisions. Looking back, you may realize that while some of the things that have hurt you were done with malicious intent, most were not.

Even those among us who are the least self-centered make their decisions with their own wellbeing and comfort in the forefront of their minds. In other words, 'Each person is the center of their own universe'. In a way, this is how it needs to be. You have to take care of yourself before you can take care of others. With that in mind realize that it is quite possible most of what has happened to hurt you wasn't done TO YOU, but because the other person was thinking of themselves, and not you. (Even if they were thinking of themselves a little too much.)

Forgive them for what happened. That does not mean what they did was ok, or that you should invite them back into your life with open arms. It just means you are not going to let it hold you back any longer.

In order to release your past hurts fully you also need to forgive yourself. People make mistakes right? You are a person and you are allowed mistakes. Forgive yourself for letting people treat you badly. Forgive yourself for treating others badly. The important thing is that you learn from what has happened, do things and make changes to reduce the chances of them happening again.

It is my opinion that God is far more interested in whom we are to become than in judging us for every misdeed we do. The battle for forgiveness is fought within one's self. The truth is when you cannot forgive yourself for something you are allowing that to have control over you. It is a subconscious block keeping you from your dreams and aspirations. You will carry it with you and be haunted by it. Forgiving yourself sets your soul free.

It is never too late to change your life. It can start with something small, or you can jump into a more drastic change. Whatever you do just don't put it off until tomorrow, Start this moment. Decide to make a change, and then make it. Try to be consistent and not fall back into old habits. Most importantly always remember if you screw up, forgive yourself and try again. Sometimes you just need to go in a different direction.

"Forgiveness will not change your past, but it will change your future."

"Gabreael"

Affirmations for this chapter:

I forgive myself, the past is gone, I focus on being the person I want to be.

I forgive those who have done me wrong, not for their sake, but for my own.

I forgive myself for the mistakes in my past.

I forgive those who have wronged me and I learn from those experiences.

Forgive and forget is easy to say,

But can you really act that way?

Forgive those who have harmed you,

Learn from what they have put you through,

Forgive yourself, for to the past you are not bound,

Mistakes have need made by all around.

11 YOUR INNER VOICE SPEAKS

Your inner voice and the inner voice of the universe work together to help you in your life.

Positivity is now being allowed in your life, you believe it should be there and that you can do anything you set your mind to. You are putting away your own ego and are open to submitting to the will of the divine, which is helping you receive its messages and act accordingly. You are manifesting which produces the things you want and need in your life. Giving Thanks has become a part of your life and it helping you to find joy and forgive yourself and others it's now time to listen to your inner voice and see what you have to say to you.

From the time I awaken in the morning until I lay my head to rest, my inner voice speaks to me. I also believe the universe has an inner voice that we draw to us based on our thoughts, and our actions. It speaks to all of us daily with environmental influences. It could be as simple as a song on the radio, a book sent your direction, meeting a person you were thinking about that you haven't seen in years, and so on.

To be able to listen to the universal inner voice you must first listen to your own inner voice. You must have confidence in and trust your intuition. You may be slightly confused as to what your inner voice is versus the universal inner voice. Think of it like this, the universal inner voice will set the message in front of you. Like making sure that a book you need to read is sticking out farther than any of the others on the shelf. It is your own inner voice that sees the book and tells you to pick it up.

Don't worry if you miss a few messages along the way. If it is important, it will show up again, over and over if needed, until you get the message. It takes practice to listen to your inner voice. At first you may second guess yourself, but try to let go of doubt and trust it.

Every day say to yourself "I am (finish the sentence) _____." By saying "I am," you become the "I am."

Back in Chapter 3, I touched on listening to the divine during your walk. This chapter will be exploring that concept more. The universal voice is all around us all the time. Most of the time it isn't necessarily trying to send you messages, but there are times when it will make its voice heard. These subtle environmental influences can show themselves in different ways.

Hitting every possible stoplight on your way somewhere could be telling you that's not where you should be going right now. However, it could be saying that you're going the wrong direction in your life in general, or simply helping you to avoid some unforeseen problem or danger ahead. Your delay could be keeping you out of an accident or argument at your destination.

Have you ever arrived somewhere and had someone say, "You just missed…"? Did you come to find out that it was something or someone you really didn't want to experience that day? This is what I'm talking about.

Maybe the exact song you needed to hear came on the radio randomly. That song also provides you with the emotional support or clarity that you need at that exact moment in time.

This can happen with books, television or movies. Some people believe the divine sends animal messengers as well, they are known as totems. Totems could fill a book alone, and there are many on the subject, so I am not going to go too deeply into them here.

You might want to take notice though if an animal starts appearing in your life on a regular basis. It might be trying to tell you something. A simple internet search can give you information about the animal (or fish, reptile or bug) in general or about it as a totem specifically.

I have stories about two people who use their environment to answer questions in their lives. Each in their own way listens to the universal voice speaking to them in a very active way. Conveniently, they are both in the same family.

I'll start with the Aunt. She was a very religious Christian. When she needed guidance or questions answered she, like many others, turned to the Bible. Unlike most she would hold the book in her hands, concentrate on the question, then open the book. Her fingers would find a random page and her eyes would go to a passage that would give her the answer she needed.

Her niece Jasmine had a different approach. She had tried to use the bible the way her aunt did, but maybe because she had never been able to connect with the book, it never worked for her.

One day she was heartbroken and took notice that the last three or four songs on the radio seemed to be exactly what she needed to hear. She realized this had happened before on other occasions. Maybe it was coincidence maybe more…

Jasmine started using the radio's seek function to answer questions. While this method did not work 100% of the time, it did seem to work a lot. She asked the cosmos to help her answer a question that had been weighing on her mind, then say, "The next song that comes on is the answer to my question," then she hit the seek button. Sometimes it took a few pushes to find a station that was both coming in clear and not on a commercial, but this method worked extremely well for her.

Here are a few things to try when learning to listen to your inner voice.

This daily meditation will help you recognize your inner voice. This one is a simple open meditation that can be done in several different ways. As with any other form start with getting relaxed, comfortable and focus on your breathing. Try to clear your mind of all thought but your breath flowing in and out, slowly and deeply.

Your second step is to inhale and exhale to a count of ten, do this about ten cycles. After that, you will probably want to move to a shorter count of six or seven whatever is comfortable, but still deeper than normal.

Once you have found a comfortable breathing cycle you start the third step. Stop counting your breaths and let you mind relax. At this point, you might start seeing pictures of having thoughts. Take not of what comes to you. Try to follow where it takes you rather than leading it. When you are ready or your time is up, start counting your breaths again. Move back to using a ten count, then move again to a sex count. Feel the chair you are sitting in, your feet firmly on the ground. Be conscious of what you hear around you and other things going on in your environment. When you are ready, open your eyes.

Think about the things you saw or heard. You may want to do a quick voice recording or write down some notes to go over later.

You can change this to answer questions as well. Once you get to the point where you are no longer counting ask a question. I could be something like, 'What should I know to help me today?' 'Is there anything I can do to help this problem or situation?'

The second exercise is a form of automatic writing. Sit down with a pen and paper. Now write. If you have something bothering you try to clear your mind first, what you are looking for are the things that just pop in.

You can also start by writing a question and then write the first answer that come to you. It could be a single word, a paragraph or pages. You may not get any answers at all. That is ok too. Your subconscious may need time to think about your questions.

The third way I am going to show you how to listen

to your inner voice is with exercise that involves both your body and your mind. People generally think of exercises like yoga, thi-chi and qigong. It may take some looking but you should be able to find classes, DVD's or online videos to help you get started.

Sometimes life gets you down, sometimes your problems are a constant knocking in your head. Using a slight alteration, you can use the second and third techniques to help you relieve this tension and ask your inner voice what to do. These are generally time-consuming processes so you will need anywhere from an hour to three or more to do either of these suggestions.

If you choose to write, get your supplies ready and if possible turn off your phone. Distractions should be limited, but background noise, especially if it relaxes you is fine. Now write. Write about whatever is bothering you. Get everything off your chest, then start looking at the problem from different angles. Turn it around in your mind as you would a trinket before you buy it. At some point during your writing, you may get insights into the situation. Thinking of things from a new prospective that you had not before can open up a new way of dealing with your problem that you didn't before.

You may have one of those Aha! Moments.

If you are generally an active person or if you are feeling very restless and agitated, this may be a better suggestion for you.

Pick your activity, it needs to be something you can do alone, that you can do on autopilot while thinking about other thing. You also need to be able to sustain the activity for at least an hour without it causing too much excursion. Possibilities are walking, running, biking etc.

Pick your direction, you can use your usually rout or an alternative one that you only use occasionally.

Regardless, it is best if you know the rout so you won't be distracted from your internal thoughts thinking about where you are going. As you take off start thinking about what is bothering you. Go over the different ideas in your mind. As with the writing, you may begin to see your problems in a new light.

Affirmations for this chapter:

I take not of the random occurrences in my life.

I listen to my inner voice.

I appreciate the small gifts from my higher power.

I am open to the subtle suggestions that are sent though my environment.

Gabreael

People are always asking for signs,

What they don't realize,

Is they are getting them all the time.

The ringing phone,

A book that falls off the shelf

These are all signs; you just have to look for yourself.

12 TIME TO WRITE YOUR STORY

It is your life, if you don't like the way it's going rewrite where you are.

Help me to see the path that lies ahead.

Help me to make the needed changes in my life.

Help me to be courageous and make these changes happen

Amen

I want you to take a few minutes. And ask yourself these questions from the deepest part of yourself. Ask yourself, "Who are you?" What do you want in life? What is or purpose in life?

I see life as a screenplay. And you are the writer. You decide how your story begins, continue and ends. If you are unhappy with the way your story is going rewrite it. The problem with many people is that they claim their story; they either don't know how to change it or don't realize they can, and they stay stuck in it. It is never too late to rewrite your story, to change the scene, the roll you are playing. When growing up my grandmother used to correct me and say, "Now you know better, now you know how to do better." This is a simple sentence from my grandmother, but it is a profound statement that changed my life.

We are often stuck in judgment of ourselves, our past history... You are not the person you were in your twenties, in your thirties, nor will you be the same person in your forties and so forth. You learn and you grow.

A chance encounter/experience changed my friend's life. She was invited out one night by a friend to see a band play at a local club. Because of some unforeseen events, Danielle ended up spending most of the evening without the friend who invited her. This was ok though because both the bands and the crowd were great.

As a result of the amazing night, Danielle realized where she wanted to be in her life. She wanted to be around fun, creative people. She realized she did not need to hide behind her friends and relationships. She was just fine all on her own. While this atmosphere could be disastrous for some, she thrived there. Danielle made great friends and learned that she really was a good and likable person.

Contrary to her worst fears, people would accept her for who she really was, and that she could be by herself and still be loved. A random invitation helped her discover where she wanted to be and she made it happen through work and determination.

During Danielle's time in this phase of her life, she gained confidence in herself and made friends and memories she would keep for a lifetime.

One of the things you were asked to do in chapter 4 was to write about your ideal life.

What I'm asking you to do now, while similar, is going to be much harder because you are going to be delving much deeper than your desires. I want you to ask yourself the hard questions about your life.

Are you happy with our life? If not, what is making you unhappy?

Are you the person you want to be? If not, what is holding you back from being that person?

Would you be proud to tell your grandparents (or a grandparent figure) about your life right now?

Would you be proud to relay the story of your life to your grandchildren?

If the answer to either of those is no, why is it?

What is the role you play in our group of friends?

Has it always been the same?

When you have those questions answered, I want you to write about the next step in your life. Write about your next phase. If your writing from chapter 4 is represent where you would like to be in 5, 10 or 2 years, this one will represent where you want to be in 6 to 18 months... Be realistic about where you want to be, but push yourself as well.

I have heard it said that you know you are taking the right steps forward if they are making you slightly uncomfortable.

Once you have the story of your next phase written, figure out what steps you need to take to get there. Then get going, your journey awaits you!

We all find ourselves stuck in our story at one time or another in the screenplay of life. Everyone who has lived has made mistakes. Get over it find forgiveness for yourself and release the inner hostage you have held so long. Pick up the pen of life and get the re-write started.

Affirmations for this chapter:

Today is the first day of the rest of my life.

How I lived in my past isn't what matters, what matters is how I live and what I do today and every day after it.

Gabreael

Worrying about the past is just a waste of time,

You can't change what happened,

You can't turn back time.

Worrying about the future,

Is futile as well,

You can't predict tomorrow,

You must wait for it as well,

Your present is made,

From how you see today,

The way you react,

To what happens on this day.

Each day is a gift,

Different from the last,

So start living each day,

In a way that makes you proud of your past.

PSALMS OF MY SOUL